Read by the poet
at the Inauguration of
William Jefferson Clinton
20 January 1993

ON THE PULSE OF MORNING

MAYA ANGELOU

ON
THE
PULSE
OF
MORNING

RANDOM HOUSE NEW YORK

ISBN 0-679-74838-5

Manufactured in the United States of America

24689753

FIRST EDITION

ON THE PULSE OF MORNING

A Rock, A River, A Tree
Hosts to species long since departed,
Marked the mastodon,
The dinosaur, who left dried tokens
Of their sojourn here
On our planet floor,
Any broad alarm of their hastening doom
Is lost in the gloom of dust and ages.

But today, the Rock cries out to us, clearly,
    forcefully,
Come, you may stand upon my
Back and face your distant destiny,

But seek no haven in my shadow,
I will give you no hiding place down here.

You, created only a little lower than
The angels, have crouched too long in
The bruising darkness
Have lain too long
Facedown in ignorance,
Your mouths spilling words

Armed for slaughter.
The Rock cries out to us today,
You may stand upon me;
But do not hide your face.

Across the wall of the world,
A River sings a beautiful song. It says,
Come, rest here by my side.

Each of you, a bordered country,
Delicate and strangely made proud,
Yet thrusting perpetually under siege.
Your armed struggles for profit
Have left collars of waste upon
My shore, currents of debris upon my breast.
Yet today I call you to my riverside,
If you will study war no more.

Come, clad in peace,
And I will sing the songs
The Creator gave to me when I and the
Tree and the Rock were one.
Before cynicism was a bloody sear across your brow
And when you yet knew you still knew nothing.
The River sang and sings on.

There is a true yearning to respond to
The singing River and the wise Rock.
So say the Asian, the Hispanic, the Jew
The African, the Native American, the Sioux,
The Catholic, the Muslim, the French, the Greek,

The Irish, the Rabbi, the Priest, the Sheik,
The Gay, the Straight, the Preacher,
The privileged, the homeless, the Teacher.
They hear. They all hear
The speaking of the Tree.

They hear the first and last of every Tree
Speak to humankind today.
Come to me,
Here beside the River.
Plant yourself beside the River.

Each of you, descendant of some passed-
On traveler, has been paid for.

You, who gave me my first name, you,
Pawnee, Apache, Seneca, you
Cherokee Nation, who rested with me, then
Forced on bloody feet,
Left me to the employment of
Other seekers—desperate for gain,
Starving for gold.

You, the Turk, the Arab, the Swede,
The German, the Eskimo, the Scot,
The Italian, the Hungarian, the Pole,
You the Ashanti, the Yoruba, the Kru, bought
Sold, stolen, arriving on a nightmare
Praying for a dream.

Here, root yourselves beside me.
I am that Tree planted by the River,
Which will not be moved.
I, the Rock, I, the River, I, the Tree
I am yours—your passages have been paid.
Lift up your faces, you have a piercing need
For this bright morning dawning for you.
History, despite its wrenching pain,
Cannot be unlived, but if faced
With courage, need not be lived again.

Lift up your eyes
Upon this day breaking for you.
Give birth again
To the dream.

ᛔ

Women, children, men,
Take it into the palms of your hands,
Mold it into the shape of your most
Private need. Sculpt it into
The image of your most public self.
Lift up your hearts
Each new hour holds new chances
For a new beginning.
Do not be wedded forever
To fear, yoked eternally
To brutishness.

∽

The horizon leans forward,

Offering you space

To place new steps of change

Here, on the pulse of this fine day

You may have the courage

To look up and out and upon me,

The Rock, the River, the Tree, your country.

No less to Midas than the mendicant.

No less to you now than the mastodon then.

∽

Here on the pulse of this new day

You may have the grace to look up and out

And into your sister's eyes,

And into your brother's face,

Your country,

And say simply

Very simply

With hope—

Good morning.

ABOUT THE AUTHOR

MAYA ANGELOU has written five volumes of autobiography, beginning with *I Know Why the Caged Bird Sings*.

She has also published five collections of poetry: *And Still I Rise, Just Give Me a Cool Drink of Water 'fore I Diiie, Oh Pray My Wings Are Gonna Fit Me Well, Shaker, Why Don't You Sing?*, and *I Shall Not Be Moved*.

ABOUT THE TYPE

This book was set in Bembo, a typeface based on an old-style Roman face that was used for Cardinal Bembo's tract *De Aetna* in 1495. Bembo was cut by Francesco Griffo in the early sixteenth century. The Lanston Monotype Machine Company of Philadelphia brought the well-proportioned letter forms of Bembo to the United States in the 1930s.